The Dominican Republic

A Peace Corps Publication

Contents

CORE EXPECTATIONS

FOR PEACE CORPS VOLUNTEERS

In working toward fulfilling the Peace Corps Mission of promoting world peace and friendship, as a trainee and Volunteer, you are expected to:

1. Prepare your personal and professional life to make a commitment to serve abroad for a full term of 27 months

2. Commit to improving the quality of life of the people with whom you live and work; and, in doing so, share your skills, adapt them, and learn new skills as needed

3. Serve where the Peace Corps asks you to go, under conditions of hardship, if necessary, and with the flexibility needed for effective service

4. Recognize that your successful and sustainable development work is based on the local trust and confidence you build by living in, and respectfully integrating yourself into, your host community and culture

5. Recognize that you are responsible 24 hours a day, 7 days a week for your personal conduct and professional performance

6. Engage with host country partners in a spirit of cooperation, mutual learning, and respect

7. Work within the rules and regulations of the Peace Corps and the local and national laws of the country where you serve

8. Exercise judgment and personal responsibility to protect your health, safety, and well-being and that of others

9. Recognize that you will be perceived, in your host country and community, as a representative of the people, cultures, values, and traditions of the United States of America

10. Represent responsively the people, cultures, values, and traditions of your host country and community to people in the United States both during and following your service

PEACE CORPS/THE DOMINICAN REPUBLIC
HISTORY AND PROGRAMS

History of the Peace Corps in the Dominican Republic

Since 1962, more than 3,000 Volunteers have served in the Dominican Republic. These Volunteers have contributed to technical skills transfer and institutional capacity-building in a wide range of fields, including agriculture, urban and rural community development, forestry, conservation, environmental education, community health and child survival, nursing, small business development, fisheries, water and sanitation, teacher education, university education, youth development, and information technology. ·

Over the years, Peace Corps Volunteers have contributed significantly to the establishment and development of many of the country's leading nongovernmental organizations (NGOs) and have worked hand-in-hand with the various administrations that have governed the Dominican Republic. In keeping with its commitment to peace and development, the Peace Corps remained in the Dominican Republic throughout its civil war in the 1960s. Our commitment to service has been highlighted through the good work of Volunteers and their project partners in the recovery efforts following two of the most severe hurricanes to hit the country's shores (David in 1979 and George in 1998).

History and Future of Peace Corps Programming in the Dominican Republic

Peace Corps/Dominican Republic provides direct, community-based technical assistance. Volunteers work in marginalized sectors of the population to promote self-help strategies that respond to basic human needs and strengthen community efforts. Currently, the 200-plus Volunteers in the Dominican Republic strive to increase local capacity for problem solving and to form links with grassroot, regional, and national organizations.

While Volunteers work primarily in community economic development, education, environment, youth development, health, and appropriate technologies, the Peace Corps' program has evolved with the country's changing needs. Innovations include the development of an "information technology for education" project; a multisector approach to programming; and the incorporation of HIV/AIDS prevention, gender and development, and youth service-learning across all projects.

Education/Information Technology for Education & Literacy

This project helps provide teacher training for the more than 600 computer centers established in public high schools around the country. Volunteers train teachers in the use of computers, focusing on how they can improve the quality of education in the classroom. Volunteers also create technology youth groups and help schools develop ways for the community to access information technology facilities. In addition, more and more Volunteers are meeting community needs by managing adult literacy programs.

Community Environmental Development

This project creates awareness among Dominicans of all ages for proper human interaction with the environment, such as appropriate waste disposal, prevention of water contamination and deforestation, soil conservation, watershed protection, protection of marine resources, appropriate energy use, preservation of air quality, noise and safety procedures, and demographic effects on the environment. To accomplish this, Volunteers help the Ministry of Environment and Ministry of Education. Volunteers develop and implement education modules that train teachers on how to incorporate environmental concepts into their curricula. They also provide training and technical support to community leaders to develop and implement projects that incorporate sound environmental practices and promote conservation projects linked to income generation, such as ecotourism around national parks and poor rural areas.

Healthy Families

The healthy families project aims to reduce the risk of infant mortality in low-income families living in rural and marginal urban communities. Volunteers are assigned to NGOs, community-based organizations, and occasionally, the Ministry of Public Health. They help health supervisors improve and sustain basic health practices and services. The project focuses on the key causes of infant mortality: diarrhea, respiratory infections, and malnutrition. Most Volunteers also help youth and health workers promote reproductive health and HIV/AIDS prevention among adolescents and young mothers.

Appropriate Technologies

The appropriate technologies sector has two tracks: water projects and appropriate technologies. Volunteers assigned to this sector seek to provide relatively inexpensive solutions to environmental, health, and economic issues faced by communities. Sample projects include improved cooking stoves, bathrooms, solar dryers, health and sanitation education programs, food processing, and gravity flow water systems. Volunteers train community members to operate and manage these projects. Like the healthy families project, this project focuses on low-income families living in rural and marginal urban communities.

Community Economic Development

Volunteers take a broad approach to fostering economic development opportunities and community capacity-building among the neediest sectors of the population. They work with farmer associations and rural community groups to develop income-generating projects in agribusiness, organize integrated community development projects, and work with nongovernmental organizations (NGOs) to provide business education to micro-entrepreneurs. Many Volunteers also provide business and leadership education to Dominican youth, using a curriculum similar to Junior Achievement's.

Youth, Families, and Community Development

The youth, families, and community development project is the most recent addition. It was initiated in 2002 to focus development activities directly toward young people as a population, and to support organizations that are working with youth development. Youth Volunteers collaborate with youth groups, community-based organizations, and nongovernmental and governmental organizations in urban, suburban, and rural areas.

The youth project seeks to empower youth by building skills and experience to make positive decisions that will affect their personal lives and their communities. Project activities include working with sports and arts, personal development training for young people, service learning, literacy support, and increasing marketable skills. The project also supports organizations that work with children and youth in extreme situations: living or working on the streets, living with HIV, being sexually exploited, victims of violence, or living in extreme poverty. The youth program integrates the five principles of positive youth development: engaging caring adults and positive role models, providing safe places and supervised activities, offering a healthy start through exercise and sex education, teaching marketable skills, and providing opportunities to serve through volunteering and engagement with the community.

COUNTRY OVERVIEW:
THE DOMINICAN REPUBLIC AT A GLANCE

History

The island of Hispaniola, of which the Dominican Republic forms the eastern two-thirds and Haiti the western one-third, has been a center of great political struggles since the arrival of Christopher Columbus in the West Indies in 1492. The island was first colonized by the Spanish, and by the end of the 17th century, Spain had ceded to France all rights to the western portion of the island.

In 1804, Toussaint L'Overture, the leader of a slave uprising in the French colony, declared the island "one and indivisible" under the new Republic of Haiti. At that time, what is now the Dominican Republic was occupied by Haitian troops. The Haitians conquered the entire island in 1822 and held it until 1844. In that year, Juan Pablo Duarte, the hero of Dominican independence, and his forces drove out the Haitians and established the Dominican Republic as an independent state.

Since independence, the country's political stability has been shaky. Economic difficulties, the threat of European intervention, and ongoing internal disorders led to a U.S. occupation in 1916 and the establishment of a military government. The occupation ended in 1924 with a democratically elected Dominican government. From 1930 until his assassination in 1961, Army Commander Rafael Trujillo ruled the country under a repressive dictatorship. The country then underwent a number of military coups, as well as an occupation by U.S. military forces from 1965 to 1966. During those years, several key political figures rose to power, including Joaquin Balaguer, leader of the Social Christian Reformist Party; and Juan Bosch, founder of the Dominican Liberation Party. Recently, the country has experienced peaceful transitions of democratically elected governments. Hipolito Mejia was elected in 2000 for a four-year term. Former President Leonel Fernandez won the 2004 election and was inaugurated in August 2004 and re-elected in 2008.

Although the Dominican Republic's relations with Haiti have been challenging, the two countries are intrinsically linked. There are a sizable number of Haitian migrants in the Dominican Republic, many of whom contribute to the Dominican economy.

The Dominican Republic has a close relationship with the United States despite the fact that America has occupied the country on two occasions. It is estimated that there are more than 1 million Dominicans living in the United States, with the majority living in New York City. The U.S. Embassy estimates that 60,000 U.S. citizens live in the Dominican Republic.

Government

The Dominican Republic is a representative democracy whose national powers are divided among independent executive, legislative, and judicial branches. The president appoints the cabinet, executes laws passed by the legislative branch, and is commander in chief of the armed forces. The president and vice president run for office on the same ticket and are elected by direct vote for four-year terms. Legislative power is exercised by a bicameral National Congress, consisting of a Senate (30 members) and a Chamber of Deputies (149 members).

There are three major political parties: the Dominican Liberation Party (PLD), led by President Leonel Fernandez; the Dominican Revolutionary Party (PRD); and the Social Christian Reformist Party (PRSC).

Economy

The Dominican Republic is a middle-income developing country. The economy is primarily dependent on services (especially tourism), remittances from the United States (which help support 30 percent of all Dominican families), construction, and agriculture. The service sector has overtaken agriculture as the leading employer of Dominicans, principally as a result of growth in tourism and free-trade zones. More than 1 million foreign tourists visit the Dominican Republic each year, contributing close to $1 billion (U.S.) to the economy.

The Dominican Republic's economic success of the 1990s has deteriorated significantly over the past few years, though it has begun to improve. The gross domestic product (GDP) fell by 1 percent in 2003 and another 1 percent in 2004; inflation grew by 60 percent in 2003 and another 35 percent in 2004. Moreover, the costs of many basic goods (gas, food, utilities) have significantly increased. However, with the administration of President Fernandez in August 2004, the economic situation began to stabilize and improve. Inflation stood at single-digit levels for 2006 and there is increasing economic growth. Additionally, the peso has been revalued and stabilized; the exchange rate is now approximately 38 pesos to $1 (U.S.).

In spite of the significant rise in prices in 2003-2004, there was no corresponding increase in wages for the working population. An average agricultural day laborer still earns approximately 150 pesos per day (less than $6 per day), and the unemployment rate is nearly 20 percent. The nation's $7 billion foreign public debt represents nearly half of its GDP. Poverty incidence in the rural areas is three times higher than in urban areas, and it reaches extreme levels on the Haitian border and in batey communities (work camps on the edge of sugar plantations in the east and along the border of the Dominican Republic and Haiti).

Severe energy shortages, with average daily blackouts of up to 12 hours, and a 60 percent increase in gas prices has had a domino effect on prices of general consumer goods and transportation. Additionally, the lack of access to potable water, inadequate access to basic preventive health services, and low pay in the service sector make it difficult for Dominicans to advance.

People and Culture
The Dominican population was 1 million in 1920; by 2007, it had grown to 9 million. The country has one of the highest population densities in the hemisphere. The population is roughly 40 percent rural and 60 percent urban.

The Dominican people are a blend of Spanish, African, and indigenous Taino Indians. The Spanish arrived in 1492; by 1520 the indigenous population had been virtually eradicated by warfare, disease, and an unsuccessful attempt to enslave them to work in the country's fields and gold mines. As the indigenous population decreased, the labor shortage was filled by African slaves brought to Santo Domingo. The current population is largely mulatto. More recently, there has been a small influx of Japanese, Chinese, European Jews, Central and South Americans, Arabs, and other groups.

The Dominican culture reflects its Spanish, African, and indigenous Indian heritages. From the Spanish, Dominicans inherited their language, cuisine, Roman Catholicism, and patriarchal family structure. From the African and indigenous Indian cultures, they inherited their music (merengue), folklore, social activities, handicrafts, cuisine, and many of the names given to children. Spanish is the official language, although many indigenous words have been incorporated into Dominican Spanish. While Roman Catholicism is the predominant religion, Christian evangelical churches are becoming a more influential religious force in the country.

Environment
The Dominican Republic has some of the most varied and beautiful terrain in the hemisphere, including mountain ranges, tropical beaches, dry forests, and desert (found primarily in the southwest.) It boasts the highest mountain in the Caribbean, Pico Duarte, which is surrounded by extremely productive farmland in the Cibao region. Sugar cane and rolling landscapes highlight southern and eastern parts of the island.

There is growing concern about the Dominican Republic's rapid rate of environmental degradation in both rural and urban areas. About 60 percent of the country's original forest cover still existed in the early 1900s. By the end of the 1980s, that figure had plunged to approximately 12 percent as a result of slash-and-burn agriculture, overgrazing, forest fires, and charcoal production. Degradation and silting in the Caribbean and Atlantic have also negatively affected the extremely rich coral reef environments found around the island.

RESOURCES FOR FURTHER INFORMATION

Following is a list of websites for additional information about the Peace Corps and the Dominican Republic and to connect you to returned Volunteers and other invitees. Please keep in mind that although we try to make sure all these links are active and current, we cannot guarantee it. If you do not have access to the Internet, visit your local library. Libraries offer free Internet usage and often let you print information to take home.

A note of caution: As you surf the Internet, be aware that you may find bulletin boards and chat rooms in which people are free to express opinions about the Peace Corps based on their own experience, including comments by those who were unhappy with their choice to serve in the Peace Corps. These opinions are not those of the Peace Corps or the U.S. government, and we hope you will keep in mind that no two people experience their service in the same way.

General Information About The Dominican Republic

www.countrywatch.com/
On this site, you can learn anything from what time it is in the capital of the Dominican Republic to how to convert from the dollar to the Dominican Republic currency. Just click on the Dominican Republic and go from there.

www.lonelyplanet.com/destinations
Visit this site for general travel advice about almost any country in the world.

www.state.gov
The State Department's website issues background notes periodically about countries around the world. Find the Dominican Republic and learn more about its social and political history. You can also go to the site's international travel section to check on conditions that may affect your safety.

www.psr.keele.ac.uk/official.htm
This includes links to all the official sites for governments worldwide.

www.geography.about.com/library/maps/blindex.htm
This online world atlas includes maps and geographical information, and each country page contains links to other sites, such as the Library of Congress, that contain comprehensive historical, social, and political background.

www.cyberschoolbus.un.org/infonation/info.asp
This United Nations site allows you to search for statistical information for member states of the U.N.

www.worldinformation.com
This site provides an additional source of current and historical information about countries around the world.

Connect With Returned Volunteers and Other Invitees

www.rpcv.org
This is the site of the National Peace Corps Association, made up of returned Volunteers. On this site you can find links to all the Web pages of the "Friends of" groups for most countries of service, comprised of former Volunteers who served in those countries. There are also regional groups that frequently get together for social events and local volunteer activities. Or go straight to the Friends of the Dominican Republic site: http://www.fotdr.org/

www.PeaceCorpsWorldwide.org
This site is hosted by a group of returned Volunteer writers. It is a monthly online publication of essays and Volunteer accounts of their Peace Corps service.

Online Articles/Current News Sites About The Dominican Republic

www.dr1.com
This site provides daily news summaries in English.

www.listin.com.do
Online edition of *Listin Diario*, a Dominican newspaper (in Spanish).

www.hoy.com.do
Online edition of *Hoy,* a Dominican newspaper (in Spanish).

www.dominicanrepublic.com/
Official Internet portal to the Dominican Republic, with information on history, culture and arts, economy, business, politics, news, etc. (in Spanish and English).

International Development Sites About The Dominican Republic

www.usaid.gov/locations/latin_america_caribbean/country/dominican_republic/
The U.S. Agency for International Development's programs in the Dominican Republic

Spanish-Learning Resources on the Web

http://www.byki.com/free_lang_software.pl
Free language learning software Before You Know It (byki), based on the flash-card system. The free version of the software contains 17 lists of words and phrases, which include sample phrases for polite conversations, meeting and greeting, and food and beverages vocabulary.

http://www.studyspanish.com/
A free Spanish tutorial, Learn Spanish provides a good opportunity for self-study. It contains lessons, audios, and exercises corrected instantly. A section of the site is free, while additional exercises are provided with a subscription.

http://www.miscositas.com/
Short stories, links, and other exercises for learning Spanish, French, and English.

http://mld.ursinus.edu/~jarana/Ejercicios/
Spanish language exercises. Materials and exercises available for students and teachers from Ursinus College, Collegeville, Penn.

Recommended Books

The first three are novels about Dominican history and the immigrant experience by a writer who moved to the United States as a girl when her parents fled the Trujillo regime.

1.   Alvarez, Julia. *How the Garcia Girls Lost Their Accents*. Chapel Hill, N.C.: Algonquin Books, 1991.

2.   Alvarez, Julia. *In the Time of the Butterflies*. Chapel Hill, N.C.: Algonquin Books, 1995.

3.   Alvarez, Julia. *¡Yo!* Chapel Hill, N.C.: Algonquin Books, 1997.

4.   Fischkin, Barbara. *Muddy Cup: A Dominican Family Comes of Age in a New America*. New York: Scribner, 1997.

A journalist follows the emigration of a Dominican family from the time they apply for visas through their move to New York.

6.   Ruck, Rob. *The Tropic of Baseball: Baseball in the Dominican Republic*. University of Nebraska Press, 1999.

Traces baseball's roots in the Dominican Republic against a historical background of economic and political change.

7.   Pons, Frank Moya. *The Dominican Republic: A National History*. New York: Hispaniola Books, 1994.

8.   Wucker, Michele. *Why the Cocks Fight: Dominicans, Haitians, and the Struggle for Hispaniola*. New York: Hill and Wang, 1999.

Books About the History of the Peace Corps
1.   Hoffman, Elizabeth Cobbs. *All You Need is Love: The Peace Corps and the Spirit of the 1960s*. Cambridge, Mass.: Harvard University Press, 2000.

2.   Rice, Gerald T. *The Bold Experiment: JFK's Peace Corps*. Notre Dame, Ind.: University of Notre Dame Press, 1985.

3.   Stossel, Scott. *Sarge: The Life and Times of Sargent Shriver*. Washington, D.C.: Smithsonian Institution Press, 2004.

4.   Meisler, Stanley. *When the World Calls: The Inside Story of the Peace Corps and its First 50 Years*. Boston, Mass.: Beacon Press, 2011.

Books on the Volunteer Experience

1.   Dirlam, Sharon. *Beyond Siberia: Two Years in a Forgotten Place*. Santa Barbara, Calif.: McSeas Books, 2004.

2.   Casebolt, Marjorie DeMoss. *Margarita: A Guatemalan Peace Corps Experience*. Gig Harbor, Wash.: Red Apple Publishing, 2000.

3.   Erdman, Sarah. *Nine Hills to Nambonkaha*: Two Years in the Heart of an African Village. New York, N.Y.: Picador, 2003.

4.   Hessler, Peter. *River Town: Two Years on the Yangtze*. New York, N.Y.: Perennial, 2001.

5.   Kennedy, Geraldine ed. *From the Center of the Earth: Stories out of the Peace Corps*. Santa Monica, Calif.: Clover Park Press, 1991.

6.   Thompsen, Moritz. *Living Poor: A Peace Corps Chronicle*. Seattle, Wash.: University of Washington Press, 1997 (reprint).

LIVING CONDITIONS AND VOLUNTEER LIFESTYLE

Communications

Mail

Mail delivery between the United States and the Dominican Republic can be unreliable. Letters and packages sent by airmail take from 10 days to several weeks to arrive. Surface mail can take months.

Your address for **regular mail** service in the Dominican Republic while you are a Peace Corps trainee (PCT) will be:

"Your Name," PCT
Cuerpo de Paz
Av Bolivar 451, Gazcue
Apartado Postal 1412
Santo Domingo, Dominican Republic

Please Note: Do not send money, airline tickets, or other valuable items through the mail.

Should you need to have a package sent to the Dominican Republic, we recommend that the contents be limited to items that fit into **padded envelopes.** These are less likely to be lost, opened, or taxed than other types of packages.

Packages may also be shipped via a parcel delivery service. Federal Express and DHL have offices in Santo Domingo. If you want them to deliver a package to the Peace Corps office, you must provide the office street address (instead of the post office box address listed above) and phone number:

Your address for **expedited mail** service in the Dominican Republic while you are a Peace Corps trainee or Volunteer will be:

"Your Name," PCT
Cuerpo de Paz
451 Avenida Bolivar
Santo Domingo, Dominican Republic
Telephone: 809.685.4102

Please Note: Federal Express and DHL will not deliver items larger than an envelope to the Peace Corps office, so **you may have to pay significant customs duties to retrieve larger items from customs**, and picking up the items may mean an entire day's travel to the capital. In addition, packages sometimes disappear in transit.

Additionally, there is a tax levied on every package received by a trainee or Volunteer. Peace Corps does not cover these costs. All packages received in-country are charged RD$100 (currently USD$2.77) for retrieval and then an additional RD$100 per pound. So, for example, a 10-pound package would cost the Volunteer RD$1,100 (USD$34.00), which is a significant amount considering a Volunteer's living allowance.

Private courier services, such as Mail Boxes Etc., provide mail-forwarding service from Miami; however, these companies are limited to major cities and receiving rates vary according to weight. While mail-forwarding services can be considered more reliable than standard surface or airmail, it can be quite costly.

During training, Peace Corps staff will deliver mail to you at least twice a week while you are in Santo Domingo; less often when you are outside of Santo Domingo. Once you move to your site, you will be responsible for sending your new mailing address to friends and family. Some Volunteers find it more convenient to continue using the Santo Domingo address. In that case, mail received at the Peace Corps office will be put in your locker in the Volunteer lounge, and you will have to collect it periodically.

We encourage you to write to your family regularly, as family members may become worried when they do not hear from you.

Telephone

The Peace Corps office in the Dominican Republic can be reached by direct dialing from the United States. The number is 1.809.685.4102. The phone number for the after-hours duty officer is 1.809.723.9944. The fax number is 1.809.689.9330.

Long-distance telephone service is available in the Dominican Republic and is not expensive. However, you may or may not have access to a land-line or cellular phone signal at your site. Therefore, **ALL Volunteers are issued cellular phones by Peace Corps/Dominican Republic**. Cellphones enable staff to maintain contact with Volunteers and to send messages in an emergency. You will be issued your phone during training. There is no charge for receiving calls or text messages on cellphones, but **all personal calls are at the Volunteers' expense.** Phone card rates for calling internationally to the U.S., Canada, or Puerto Rico are typically the same as making a local call. Prepaid calling cards bought in the United States typically don't work. Volunteers may use call centers of the major telephone companies, which have branches throughout the country. During training, you may or may not have access to a telephone. During your first days in-country you will be placed with a host family and will be able to assess the communication systems available to you. Please inform your family and friends that you will not be able to confirm telephone communication for at least three days after your arrival to the Dominican Republic.

Computer, Internet, and Email Access

If your sponsoring agency or project partner owns a computer, you may be able to arrange access for work-related or personal use. The resource center and computer room at the Peace Corps office in Santo Domingo has a limited number of computers with Internet access for Volunteer use. However, if you want to receive personal email, you will need to set up an account with a service such as Yahoo!, Hotmail, or Gmail. Internet access is also available at Internet cafes throughout the country. Peace Corps staff computers are not available for Volunteer use. For those with laptops, wireless services are available at the Peace Corps office, training center, and larger shopping centers in the cities; however, **service can be unreliable and unpredictable**. We highly suggest that Volunteers bring laptops if possible; they can enhance the Volunteer's work in many ways. If you do plan on bringing a laptop or any other valuable electronic equipment (cameras, Ipods, etc.) please purchase personal article insurance as theft is a serious issue in the county. Insurance may be purchased at http://www.clements.com

Housing and Site Location

During pre-service training (PST), you will live with two different Dominican host families. One will be located in the northern barrios or Santo Domingo, close to the training center. During the community-based technical training (weeks 3-8 of PST), you will live with another family in the interior of the country where your technical training program takes place. The families are selected by training staff. Houses in Santo Domingo typically have electricity and running water (when these systems are operating). Houses in the interior communities (your CBT family) frequently have little access to electricity and water; however, this will depend greatly on your program and the nature of the technical training. Your host family will provide you with a private room, and you will eat your meals with the family.

You will also live with a host family during the first three months of your Volunteer service. These host families are identified by the community and/or the host country agency and are approved by Peace Corps staff prior to your arrival. Living with a Dominican family allows faster integration into the community, provides a safe environment while you are settling in, and gives you time to look for independent housing should you choose to do so. It is important to understand that Peace Corps cannot guarantee that Volunteers will find independent housing after the initial three-month period of living with a host family. Due to a general shortage of quality housing options in the small communities where Volunteer live and work, many Volunteers often find that living with a host family for longer than three months is the norm. During service, you are expected to live in the same type of housing commonly found in your community. Housing varies widely, depending on whether you live in a city, a large or small town, or a *campo* (rural) village

Volunteers typically live in houses with tin roofs, walls of wood or cement block, and cement floors. Many communities have electricity, though some do not. Power outages are very common. The water supply is subject to the same inconsistencies. Many communities do not have water piped into houses. Rural families, for example, often have to walk to the nearest river or other water source for household water. Even if you live in a house with faucets, there is no guarantee that there will be water; it is common for water not to appear for days at a time. Volunteers placed in towns and more urbanized areas will also face some of these same challenges.

Living Allowance and Money Management

As a Volunteer, you will receive a monthly living allowance in the local currency (Dominican pesos; abbreviated as RD). The living allowance is meant to cover housing, utilities, household supplies, normal clothing replacement, food, transportation, moderate entertainment expenses, reading material, and incidentals. It will enable you to live modestly, at the same level as your neighbors and colleagues. Peace Corps/Dominican Republic will open a bank account for you and provide you with an ATM card. You will need to budget appropriately to make the living allowance last a month.

Additionally, you will receive a monthly vacation allowance equivalent to $24, paid in local currency at the same time as the living allowance. You will also receive a one-time settling-in allowance to purchase needed household furniture and equipment (e.g., a bed, a stove, kitchen items, and locks) and pay several months of advance rent if required.

Most Volunteers find they can live comfortably in the Dominican Republic with these allowances, so we strongly discourage you from supplementing the living allowance with money from home. Still, many Volunteers bring money from home for out-of-country travel. Credit cards can be used in many establishments in major cities and traveler's checks can be cashed for a small fee.

Food and Diet

The Dominican diet consists primarily of rice, beans, yuca (cassava), plantains, sweet potatoes, potatoes, and other vegetables, along with eggs, chicken, pork, beef, and some fish. The national dish is sancocho, a rich vegetable-and-meat stew served on special occasions. A typical Dominican meal, called *la bandera*, is a mix of rice, red beans, and meat. Yuca may be boiled, prepared as fritters, or baked into rounds of crisp cracker bread called casabe. Most dishes are not spicy. Locally grown, seasonal fruits include bananas, mangoes, papayas, pineapples, guavas, and avocados. Dominicans generally eat small quantities of meat at meals. Bacalau (dried fish; usually cod) can be found in several areas, but fresh fish is generally available only along the coast. Habichuelas con dulce, a sweet desert made from beans, is popular at Easter.

Vegetarians will be able to maintain their diet at home, but they will be offered—and most likely expected to accept—traditional foods, including meat, when visiting Dominican families. You will have to be open and flexible about sharing in the Dominican diet when necessary.

During training, your host family will provide your meals. Once you are at your site, you can choose to eat with Dominicans or cook on your own. To supplement their diet, some Volunteers plant gardens at home.

Transportation

Transportation is relatively easy in the Dominican Republic. Most urban travel is by bus and van, although *carro públicos* (a sort of shared taxi) are available as well. Intercity travel is by bus, while rural travel runs the gamut—from air-conditioned minibuses to crowded carro públicos, to lots of walking. Although inexpensive, carro públicos are where most Volunteers experience pick-pocketing and robberies. For security purposes. Peace Corps/Dominican Republic does not allow Volunteers or trainees to use public transportation between the hours of 7 p.m. and 7 a.m. Private taxis must be used at night.

Peace Corps Volunteers are not allowed to drive vehicles or motorcycles in the Dominican Republic. Violation of this policy will result in termination of your Peace Corps service.

Most Volunteers rely on public transportation to get around, but Volunteers can request assistance from the Peace Corps in arranging alternative means of local transportation. Volunteers can apply for and receive limited funds from their Volunteer readjustment allowance to purchase a bicycle to use during their service in the Dominican Republic. The Peace Corps will also provide you with a helmet, which you must wear at all times while riding a bicycle. Failure to abide by this policy will also result in termination of your Peace Corps service.

Climate

With an average temperature range of 65 to 95 degrees Fahrenheit, this Caribbean country is probably not as hot as you might think. It is difficult to define a rainy season, since showers can occur at any time during the year, depending on the area. However, the period of heaviest rainfall for most of the island is late April to early October, months that can be relatively hot and humid. The cooler season—from November to February—is pleasant but still warm, with temperatures from 65 F to 85 F. You will need both lightweight clothing suitable for hot weather and at least one heavier garment for traveling to cooler, mountainous areas such as the 10,000-foot Pico Duarte, the highest mountain in the Caribbean.

Social Activities

Social activities in the Dominican Republic vary depending on where you are located. They include taking part in festivities such as Carnival, parties, and dances. Some Volunteers visit other nearby Volunteers on weekends for work-related or social occasions and will make an occasional trip to the capital. We encourage Volunteers to remain at their sites as much as possible to help accomplish the Peace Corps' goal of cultural exchange. Most regional capitals have cafés and restaurants, movie theaters, and other forms of entertainment.

Social life in the Dominican Republic often revolves around the family porch, where people talk while playing dominoes, a national pastime. Outdoor tables in front of homes, bars, and *colmados* (neighborhood markets) are surrounded by men who play for hours, especially on Sundays. Outdoor players are almost exclusively men, but everyone plays at home. Even young children become adept at the game. Baseball is the country's most popular sport. The competition is keen, and rarely does a day go by when children, youth, and even adults are not playing baseball with anything they can find to use as a bat and ball. Cockfighting is another national pastime, and the gambling stakes can be high.

Dominicans also love music and dancing. *Merengue* is the national dance, and many people, including small children, know the steps. The fast-paced, rhythmic music of merengue is traditionally performed with three instruments: a *tambora* (a small drum), a *melodeon* (similar to an accordion), and a *guira* (a scraping percussion instrument). *Bachata* is another folk dance that has become just as popular as merengue. Salsa and other styles of Latin American music are popular, as are North American pop and jazz. Discos exist even in rural communities.

What has kept merengue alive over the years is its place in the Dominican Republic's Carnival celebrations. All of the major cities celebrate Carnival with zeal, incorporating music and dance into street parades and other festivities. In Santo Domingo, Carnival occurs twice a year. The first occurs during the traditional pre-Lenten holiday. The second one, much smaller but just as festive, starts the day before August 16, which is the anniversary of the Dominican Republic's declaration of war against Spain in 1863.

Each July, Santo Domingo hosts a merengue festival along its main seaside strip, *El Malecón*. The street is closed off to make way for some of the country's most popular bands. Celebrations also take place at clubs, hotels, and even nighttime beach parties. Smaller merengue festivals take place in other towns.

Professionalism, Dress, and Behavior

Dominicans take pride in their personal appearance. To gain the acceptance, respect, and confidence of rural, urban, and government-level workers, it is essential that you dress and conduct yourself professionally. Standards of dress for development professionals tends to be conservative. Women are expected to wear casual pants or mid-length skirts for professional activities (excluding physical labor) and men are expected to wear pants for professional activities other than sports and physical labor. Simply stated, first impressions will be informed by the way you dress. Establishing yourself as a professional technical resource in your community is a part of the overall challenge of adjusting to a new language and culture. Dressing as a professional will ease this process for you. Inappropriate dress may send unintended messages or invitations to co-workers and/or others in your community.

Out of respect for Dominican culture, Volunteers are not allowed to display body piercings. This includes nose rings, tongue bolts, and navel rings. Men are not allowed to wear earrings or have long hair or ponytails. If you do not remove your body rings and cut your hair before you arrive in the Dominican Republic, you will be asked to do so before you move in with a host family during training. Adherence to this policy is an important test of your motivation and commitment to adapt to the new environment. If you have reservations about this policy and the degree of sacrifice and flexibility required to be a successful Volunteer, you should re-evaluate your decision to accept the invitation to Peace Corps/Dominican Republic.

The Peace Corps expects you to comport yourself in a way that will foster respect in your community and reflect well on the Peace Corps and on citizens of the United States. Drinking and smoking in public is strongly discouraged as Volunteers are seen as role models, especially among local youth. You will receive an orientation on appropriate behavior and cultural sensitivity during pre-service training. As a Volunteer, you have the status of an invited guest and must be sensitive to the habits, tastes, and taboos of your hosts. Behavior that jeopardizes the Peace Corps' mission in the Dominican Republic or your personal safety could lead to an administrative separation—a termination of your Peace Corps service. The *Peace Corps Volunteer Handbook* has more information on the grounds for administrative separation.

Personal Safety

More detailed information about the Peace Corps' approach to safety is contained in the "Health Care and Safety" chapter, but it is an important issue and cannot be overemphasized. As stated in the *Volunteer Handbook*, becoming a Peace Corps Volunteer entails certain safety risks. Living and traveling in an unfamiliar environment (oftentimes alone), having a limited understanding of local language and culture, and being perceived as well-off are some of the factors that can put a Volunteer at risk. Many Volunteers experience varying degrees of unwanted attention and harassment. Petty thefts and burglaries are not uncommon, and incidents of physical and sexual assault do occur, although most the Dominican Republic Volunteers complete their two years of service without incident. The Peace Corps has established procedures and policies designed to help you reduce your risks and enhance your safety and security. These procedures and policies, in addition to safety training, will be provided once you arrive in the Dominican Republic. Using these tools, you are expected to take responsibility for your safety and well-being.

Each staff member at the Peace Corps is committed to providing Volunteers with the support they need to successfully meet the challenges they will face to have a safe, healthy, and productive service. We encourage Volunteers and families to look at our safety and security information on the Peace Corps website at **www.peacecorps.gov/safety**

Information on these pages gives messages on Volunteer health and Volunteer safety. There is a section titled "Safety and Security in Depth." Among topics addressed are the risks of serving as a Volunteer, posts' safety support systems, and emergency planning and communications.

During training we will discuss with you the risks and strategies for staying safe; however, please be advised that theft is quite common. We strongly advise all trainees and Volunteers to purchase personal article insurance (Clements International http://www.clements.com/expatriate/overview.asp).

Rewards and Frustrations

Although the potential for job satisfaction in the Dominican Republic is quite high, like all Volunteers, you will encounter frustrations. Because of financial or other challenges, collaborating agencies do not always provide the support promised. In addition, the pace of work and life is slower than what most Americans are accustomed to, and some people you work with may be hesitant to change practices and traditions that are centuries old. For these reasons, the Peace Corps experience of adapting to a new culture and environment is often described as a series of emotional peaks and valleys.

You will be given a high degree of responsibility and independence in your work, perhaps more than in any other job you have had or will have. You will often find yourself in situations that require an ability to motivate yourself and your co-workers with little guidance from supervisors. You might work for months without seeing any visible impact from, or without receiving feedback on, your work. Development is a slow process. Positive progress most often comes after the combined efforts of several Volunteers over the course of many years. You must possess the self-confidence, patience, and vision to continue working toward long-term goals without seeing immediate results.

To overcome these difficulties, you will need maturity, flexibility, open-mindedness, and resourcefulness. The Peace Corps staff, your co-workers, and fellow Volunteers will support you during times of challenge as well as in moments of success. Judging by the experience of former Volunteers, the peaks are well worth the difficult times, and most Volunteers leave the Dominican Republic feeling that they gained much more than they gave during their service. If you are able to make the commitment to integrate into your community and work hard, you will be a successful Volunteer.

Volunteers usually are readily accepted by their host community and make lasting friendships. However, for many Volunteers, constantly being asked personal questions, the lack of privacy, being considered a rich foreigner, and the need to be aware of different social mores can be trying. As in most Latin American countries, women in the Dominican Republic do not have the freedoms to which North American women are accustomed. A female Volunteer's inability to adapt to this reality can make her less effective and possibly even affect her safety.

The Peace Corps is not for everyone. Creativity, initiative, flexibility, patience, and a high tolerance for ambiguity are necessary attributes in confronting the challenges associated with facilitating change in a cultural setting different from the United States. Your dedication, however, can have real and lasting results. When your service is over, you will have the deep satisfaction of having played a role in a grassroots development process that helped give Dominicans greater control of their future.

PEACE CORPS TRAINING

Overview of Pre-Service Training

Training is an essential part of Peace Corps service. Our goal is to give you the skills and information necessary to live and work effectively in the Dominican Republic. In doing so, we build upon the experiences and expertise you bring to the Peace Corps. We anticipate that you will approach training with an open mind, a desire to learn, and a willingness to become involved. Trainees officially become Peace Corps Volunteers after successful completion of training.

You will participate in 10 weeks of intensive training in five major areas: technical job orientation, language (Spanish), cross-cultural adaptation, health, and safety training. You will live in a community near Santo Domingo with a Dominican family, sharing meals, conversations, and other everyday experiences. You will also visit secondary towns and rural areas to get accustomed to the realities of life in the Dominican Republic. Trainees are together for the first 3 1/2 weeks of training. For five weeks, you will live in a smaller town for community-based training by project sector. Following the community-based portion of your training, you will travel to your future project site for an orientation visit and then return to the capital for a training wrap-up and to swear in as a Peace Corps Volunteer. If you are serving with a spouse and you and your spouse are assigned to different programs, you will live apart for the community-based training portion of the program. Married couples are allowed to get together for one weekend during community-based training if they are in different project areas.

Training helps you learn how to apply your strengths and knowledge to new situations, developing your skills as a facilitator in a variety of technical areas. It doesn't make you an expert. At the onset of training, the training staff will outline the goals you must achieve to become a Volunteer and the criteria that will be used to assess your progress. (A detailed breakdown of these criteria will be provided in-country.) Evaluation of your performance during training consists of a continual dialogue between you and the training staff.

Technical Training

Technical training will prepare you to work in the Dominican Republic by building on the skills you already have and helping you develop new skills in a manner appropriate to the needs of the country. The Peace Corps staff, Dominican Republic experts, and current Volunteers will conduct the training program. Training places great emphasis on learning how to transfer the skills you have to the community in which you will serve as a Volunteer.

Technical training will include sessions on the general economic and political environment in the Dominican Republic and strategies for working within such a framework. You will review your technical sector's goals and will meet with the Dominican Republic agencies and organizations that invited the Peace Corps to assist them. You will be supported and evaluated throughout the training to build the confidence and skills you need to undertake your project activities and be a productive member of your community.

Your technical training will mainly be carried out during the community-based (weeks 3-8 of PST) portion of training. During this time, you will train only with those individuals assigned to the same sector. Trainees and staff will travel to the CBT community and live with host families during this portion of training. The training will be specific to your technical sector and provide you with the opportunity to carry out learning objectives in the local context and through collaborating with local community members.

Language Training

As a Peace Corps Volunteer, you will find that language skills are key to personal and professional satisfaction during your service. These skills are critical to your job performance, they help you integrate into your community, and they can ease your personal adaptation to the new surroundings. Therefore, language training is at the heart of the training program. You must successfully meet minimum language requirements to complete training and become a Volunteer. Dominican Republic language instructors teach formal language classes five days a week in small groups of four to five people.

Your language training will incorporate a community-based approach. In addition to classroom time, you will be given assignments to work on outside of the classroom and with your host family. The goal is to get you to a point of basic social communication skills so you can practice and develop language skills further once you are at your site. Prior to being sworn in as a Volunteer, you will work on strategies to continue language studies during your service.

Cross-Cultural Training

As part of your pre-service training, you will live with a Dominican Republic host family. This experience is designed to ease your transition to life at your site. Families go through an orientation conducted by training staff to explain the purpose of pre-service training and to assist them in helping you adapt to living in the Dominican Republic. Many Volunteers form strong and lasting friendships with their host families.

Cross-cultural and community development training will help you improve your communication skills and understand your role as a facilitator of development. You will be exposed to topics such as community mobilization, conflict resolution, gender and development, nonformal and adult education strategies, and political structures.

Health Training

During pre-service training, you will be given basic medical training and information. You will be expected to practice preventive health care and to take responsibility for your own health by adhering to all medical policies. Trainees are required to attend all medical sessions. The topics include preventive health measures and minor and major medical issues that you might encounter while in the Dominican Republic. Nutrition, mental health, setting up a safe living compound, and how to avoid HIV/AIDS and other sexually transmitted diseases (STDs) are also covered.

Safety Training

During the safety training sessions, you will learn how to adopt a lifestyle that reduces your risks at home, at work, and during your travels. You will also learn appropriate, effective strategies for coping with unwanted attention and about your individual responsibility for promoting safety throughout your service.

Additional Trainings During Volunteer Service

In its commitment to institutionalize quality training, the Peace Corps has implemented a training system that provides Volunteers with continual opportunities to examine their commitment to Peace Corps service while increasing their technical and cross-cultural skills. During service, there are usually three training events. The titles and objectives for those trainings are as follows:

- In-service training: *Provides an opportunity for Volunteers to upgrade their technical, language, and project development skills while sharing their experiences and reaffirming their commitment after having served for three to six months.*

- Midterm conference (done in conjunction with technical sector in-service): *Assists Volunteers in reviewing their first year, reassessing their personal and project objectives, and planning for their second year of service.*

- Close of service conference: *Prepares Volunteers for the future after Peace Corps service and reviews their respective projects and personal experiences.*

The number, length, and design of these trainings are adapted to country-specific needs and conditions. The key to the training system is that training events are integrated and interrelated, from the pre-departure orientation through the end of your service, and are planned, implemented, and evaluated cooperatively by the training staff, Peace Corps staff, and Volunteers.

YOUR HEALTH CARE AND SAFETY IN THE DOMINICAN REPUBLIC

The Peace Corps' highest priority is maintaining the good health and safety of every Volunteer. Peace Corps medical programs emphasize the preventive, rather than the curative, approach to disease. The Peace Corps in the Dominican Republic maintains a clinic with a full-time medical officer, who takes care of Volunteers' primary health care needs. Additional medical services, such as testing and basic treatment, are also available in the Dominican Republic at local hospitals. If you become seriously ill, you will be transported either to an American-standard medical facility in the region or to the United States.

Health Issues in the Dominican Republic

Major health problems among Volunteers in the Dominican Republic are rare and are often the result of a Volunteer not taking preventive measures to stay healthy. The most common health problems in the country are minor ones that are also found in the United States, such as colds, diarrhea, sinus infections, skin infections, headaches, dental problems, sexually transmitted illnesses (STIs), adjustment disorders, and alcohol abuse. These problems may be more frequent or compounded by life in the Dominican Republic because certain environmental factors here raise the risk or exacerbate the severity of illnesses and injuries.

The most common major health problems are dengue fever, malaria, amoebic dysentery, and HIV/AIDS. Because malaria is endemic in the Dominican Republic, taking antimalarial pills is required. You will receive vaccinations against the following: hepatitis A, hepatitis B, meningococcal meningitis, rabies, typhoid, MMR (measles, mumps, and rubella), flu vaccine, and TD (tetanus and diphtheria). If you have already received any of these vaccinations, please bring written documentation of the dates they were administered.

Amoebic dysentery can be avoided by thoroughly washing fruits and vegetables and either boiling drinking water or using the water purification tablets provided in your Peace Corps-issued medical kit.

Helping You Stay Healthy

The Peace Corps will provide you with all the necessary inoculations, medications, and information to stay healthy. Upon your arrival in the Dominican Republic, you will receive a medical handbook. At the end of training, you will receive a medical kit with supplies to take care of mild illnesses and first aid needs. The contents of the kit are listed later in this chapter.

During pre-service training, you will have access to basic medical supplies through the medical officer. However, you will be responsible for your own supply of prescription drugs and any other specific medical supplies you require, as the Peace Corps will not order these items during training. Please bring a three-month supply of any prescription drugs you use, since they may not be available here and it may take several months for shipments to arrive.

You will have physicals at midservice and at the end of your service. If you develop a serious medical problem during your service, the medical officer in the Dominican Republic will consult with the Office of Medical Services in Washington, D.C. If it is determined that your condition cannot be treated in the Dominican Republic, you may be sent out of the country for further evaluation and care.

Maintaining Your Health

As a Volunteer, you must accept considerable responsibility for your own health. Proper precautions will significantly reduce your risk of serious illness or injury. The adage "An ounce of prevention ..." becomes extremely important in areas where diagnostic and treatment facilities are not up to the standards of the United States.

Many illnesses that afflict Volunteers worldwide are entirely preventable if proper food and water precautions are taken. These illnesses include food poisoning, parasitic infections, hepatitis A, dysentery, Guinea worms, tapeworms, and typhoid fever. Your medical officer will discuss specific standards for water and food preparation in the Dominican Republic during pre-service training.

Abstinence is the only certain choice for preventing infection with HIV and other sexually transmitted diseases. You are taking risks if you choose to be sexually active. To lessen risk, use a condom every time you have sex. Whether your partner is a host country citizen, a fellow Volunteer, or anyone else, do not assume this person is free of HIV/AIDS or other STDs. You will receive more information from the medical officer about this important issue.

Volunteers are expected to adhere to an effective means of birth control to prevent an unplanned pregnancy. Your medical officer can help you decide on the most appropriate method to suit your individual needs. Contraceptive methods are available without charge from the medical officer.

It is critical to your health that you promptly report to the medical office or other designated facility for scheduled immunizations, and that you let the medical officer know immediately of significant illnesses and injuries.

Women's Health Information

Pregnancy is treated in the same manner as other Volunteer health conditions that require medical attention but also have programmatic ramifications. The Peace Corps is responsible for determining the medical risk and the availability of appropriate medical care if the Volunteer remains in-country. Given the circumstances under which Volunteers live and work in Peace Corps countries, it is rare that the Peace Corps' medical and programmatic standards for continued service during pregnancy can be met.

If feminine hygiene products are not available for you to purchase on the local market, the Peace Corps medical officer in the Dominican Republic will provide them. If you require a specific product, please bring a three-month supply with you.

Your Peace Corps Medical Kit

The Peace Corps medical officer will provide you with a kit that contains basic items necessary to prevent and treat illnesses that may occur during service. Kit items can be periodically restocked at the medical office.

Medical Kit Contents

Ace bandages

Adhesive tape

American Red Cross First Aid & Safety Handbook

Antacid tablets (Tums)

Antibiotic ointment (Bacitracin/Neomycin/Polymycin B)

Antiseptic antimicrobial skin cleaner (Hibiclens)

Band-Aids

Butterfly closures

Calamine lotion

Cepacol lozenges

Condoms

Dental floss

Diphenhydramine HCL 25 mg (Benadryl)

Insect repellent stick (Cutter's)

Iodine tablets (for water purification)

Lip balm (Chapstick)

Oral rehydration salts

Oral thermometer (Fahrenheit)

Pseudoephedrine HCL 30 mg (Sudafed)

Robitussin-DM lozenges (for cough)

Scissors

Sterile gauze pads

Tetrahydrozaline eyedrops (Visine)

Tinactin (antifungal cream)

Tweezers

Before You Leave: A Medical Checklist

If there has been any change in your health—physical, mental, or dental—since you submitted your examination reports to the Peace Corps, you must immediately notify the Office of Medical Services. Failure to disclose new illnesses, injuries, allergies, or pregnancy can endanger your health and may jeopardize your eligibility to serve.

If your dental exam was done more than a year ago, or if your physical exam is more than two years old, contact the Office of Medical Services to find out whether you need to update your records. If your dentist or

Peace Corps dental consultant has recommended that you undergo dental treatment or repair, you must complete that work and make sure your dentist sends requested confirmation reports or X-rays to the Office of Medical Services.

If you wish to avoid having duplicate vaccinations, contact your physician's office to obtain a copy of your immunization record and bring it to your pre-departure orientation. If you have any immunizations prior to Peace Corps service, the Peace Corps cannot reimburse you for the cost. The Peace Corps will provide all the immunizations necessary for your overseas assignment, either at your pre-departure orientation or shortly after you arrive in the Dominican Republic. You do not need to begin taking malaria medication prior to departure.

Bring a three-month supply of any prescription or over-the-counter medication you use on a regular basis, including birth control pills. Although the Peace Corps cannot reimburse you for this three-month supply, it will order refills during your service. While awaiting shipment—which can take several months—you will be dependent on your own medication supply. The Peace Corps will not pay for herbal or nonprescribed medications, such as St. John's wort, glucosamine, selenium, or antioxidant supplements.

You are encouraged to bring copies of medical prescriptions signed by your physician. This is not a requirement, but they might come in handy if you are questioned in transit about carrying a three-month supply of prescription drugs.

If you wear eyeglasses, bring two pairs with you—a pair and a spare. If a pair breaks, the Peace Corps will replace them, using the information your doctor in the United States provided on the eyeglasses form during your examination. The Peace Corps discourages you from using contact lenses during your service to reduce your risk of developing a serious infection or other eye disease. Most Peace Corps countries do not have appropriate water and sanitation to support eye care with the use of contact lenses. The Peace Corps will not supply or replace contact lenses or associated solutions unless an ophthalmologist has recommended their use for a specific medical condition and the Peace Corps' Office of Medical Services has given approval.

If you are eligible for Medicare, are over 50 years of age, or have a health condition that may restrict your future participation in health care plans, you may wish to consult an insurance specialist about unique coverage needs before your departure. The Peace Corps will provide all necessary health care from the time you leave for your pre-departure orientation until you complete your service. When you finish, you will be entitled to the post-service health care benefits described in the Peace Corps *Volunteer Handbook*. You may wish to consider keeping an existing health plan in effect during your service if you think age or pre-existing conditions might prevent you from re-enrolling in your current plan when you return home.

Safety and Security—Our Partnership

Serving as a Volunteer overseas entails certain safety and security risks. Living and traveling in an unfamiliar environment, a limited understanding of the local language and culture, and the perception of being a wealthy American are some of the factors that can put a Volunteer at risk. Property theft and burglaries are not uncommon. Incidents of physical and sexual assault do occur, although almost all Volunteers complete their two years of service without serious personal safety problems.

Beyond knowing that Peace Corps approaches safety and security as a partnership with you, it might be helpful to see how this partnership works. Peace Corps has policies, procedures, and training in place to promote your safety. We depend on you to follow those policies and to put into practice what you have learned. An example of how this works in practice—in this case to help manage the risk of burglary—is:

- Peace Corps assesses the security environment where you will live and work

- Peace Corps inspects the house where you will live according to established security criteria

- Peace Corp provides you with resources to take measures such as installing new locks

- Peace Corps ensures you are welcomed by host country authorities in your new community

- Peace Corps responds to security concerns that you raise

- You lock your doors and windows

- You adopt a lifestyle appropriate to the community where you live

- You get to know neighbors

- You decide if purchasing personal articles insurance is appropriate for you

- You don't change residences before being authorized by Peace Corps

- You communicate concerns that you have to Peace Corps staff

This *Welcome Book* contains sections on: Living Conditions and Volunteer Lifestyle; Peace Corps Training; and Your Health Care and Safety that all include important safety and security information to help you understand this partnership. The Peace Corps makes every effort to give Volunteers the tools they need to function in the safest way possible, because working to maximize the safety and security of Volunteers is our highest priority. Not only do we provide you with training and tools to prepare for the unexpected, but we teach you to identify, reduce, and manage the risks you may encounter.

Factors that Contribute to Volunteer Risk

There are several factors that can heighten a Volunteer's risk, many of which are within the Volunteer's control. By far the most common crime that Volunteers experience is theft. Thefts often occur when Volunteers are away from their sites, in crowded locations (such as markets or on public transportation), and when leaving items unattended.

Before you depart for the Dominican Republic there are several measures you can take to reduce your risk:

- Leave valuable objects in U.S.

- Leave copies of important documents and account numbers with someone you trust in the U.S.

- Purchase a hidden money pouch or "dummy" wallet as a decoy

- Purchase personal articles insurance

After you arrive in the Dominican Republic, you will receive more detailed information about common crimes, factors that contribute to Volunteer risk, and local strategies to reduce that risk. For example, Volunteers in the Dominican Republic learn to:

- Choose safe routes and times for travel, and travel with someone trusted by the community whenever possible

- Make sure one's personal appearance is respectful of local customs

- Avoid high-crime areas

- Know the local language to get help in an emergency

- Make friends with local people who are respected in the community

- Limit alcohol consumption

As you can see from this list, you must be willing to work hard and adapt your lifestyle to minimize the potential for being a target for crime. As with anywhere in the world, crime does exist in the Dominican Republic. You can reduce your risk by avoiding situations that place you at risk and by taking precautions. Crime at the village or town level is less frequent than in the large cities; people know each other and generally are less likely to steal from their neighbors. Tourist attractions in large towns are favorite worksites for pickpockets.

The following are other security concerns in The Dominican Republic of which you should be aware:

- Location: Most crimes occurred when Volunteers were in public areas (e.g., street, park, beach, public buildings). Specifically, 43 percent of assaults took place when Volunteers were away from their sites.

- Time of day: Assaults usually took place on the weekend during the evening between 5 p.m. and 2 a.m. — with most assaults occurring around 1 a.m.

- Absence of others: Assaults usually occurred when the Volunteer was unaccompanied. In 82 percent of sexual assaults the Volunteer was unaccompanied and in 55 percent of physical assaults the Volunteer was unaccompanied.

- Relationship to assailant: In most assaults, the Volunteer did not know the assailant.

- Consumption of alcohol: Forty percent of all assaults involved alcohol consumption by Volunteers and/or assailants.

- Motor vehicle accidents

These are the single greatest risk to your safety in the Dominican Republic. Volunteers are required to wear helmets at all times while riding motorcycles. You are strongly encouraged to wear seat belts whenever available and to avoid riding in overcrowded public buses or vans. Volunteers are not allowed to drive motorized vehicles and are prohibited from traveling long distances in cars or buses at night. When you travel for official business, the Peace Corps will reimburse your expenses for bus or airline tickets.

Robbery/burglary

Some Volunteers' homes have been robbed in the past, so you need to exercise the same precautions that you would in the United States. The Peace Corps will provide information on proper home safety during training and requires landlords to install proper locks on all Volunteer housing. In addition, many Americans and Dominicans have been the victims of muggings, especially in Santo Domingo.

A common strategy of muggers is for a man to walk up behind a person and grab his or her cellphone, bag, or purse, making a getaway on a motorcycle driven by a partner. It is, therefore, important to travel on well-lit streets at night with other people around you.

Border conflicts

Dominicans and Haitians have had border conflicts in the past. At times, the disputes have resulted in gunfire and the involvement of the military. For safety reasons, travel to Haiti is currently prohibited.

Harassment

Volunteers have reported varying levels of harassment, such as sexual comments and being called derogatory names, though this rarely happens at Volunteers' sites, where they are known. Strategies for dealing and coping with harassment will be discussed during pre-service training.

Alcohol abuse

The Dominican Republic has a higher rate of alcoholism than the United States. Volunteers have reported being approached by drunken men asking for money and alcohol. It is best to avoid frequenting bars, particularly at night. Alcohol use impairs judgment and must be consumed responsibly. The Peace Corps does not tolerate public drunkenness by Volunteers, which can lead to termination of their service.

Sexual assault

Volunteers have been targets of sexual assault in the Dominican Republic. Alcohol consumption and cross-cultural differences in gender relations often are associated with sexual assaults. In those cases when the Volunteer did not know the assailant, the Volunteer was able to get out of the situation, preventing the rape. Volunteers who take seriously the training provided by the Peace Corps regarding sexual assaults will minimize their risk. Volunteers are urged to report all assaults and threats of assault to the Peace Corps medical officer so staff can respond with appropriate support. (Note that sex outside of marriage is not looked upon favorably in the Dominican Republic and that promiscuous behavior on your part may jeopardize your safety or your ability to develop mutually respectful relationships in your community and your job).

While whistles and exclamations may be fairly common on the street, this behavior can be reduced if you dress conservatively, abide by local cultural norms, and respond according to the training you will receive.

Staying Safe: Don't Be a Target for Crime

You must be prepared to take on a large degree of responsibility for your own safety. You can make yourself less of a target, ensure that your home is secure, and develop relationships in your community that will make you an unlikely victim of crime. While the factors that contribute to your risk in The Dominican Republic may be different, in many ways you can do what you would do if you moved to a new city anywhere: Be cautious, check things out, ask questions, learn about your neighborhood, know where the more risky locations are, use common sense, and be aware. You can reduce your vulnerability to crime by integrating into your community, learning the local language, acting responsibly, and abiding by Peace Corps policies and procedures. Serving safely and effectively in The Dominican Republic will require that you accept some restrictions on your current lifestyle.

Support from Staff

If a trainee or Volunteer is the victim of a safety incident, Peace Corps staff is prepared to provide support. All Peace Corps posts have procedures in place to respond to incidents of crime committed against Volunteers. The first priority for all posts in the aftermath of an incident is to ensure the Volunteer is safe and receiving medical treatment as needed. After assuring the safety of the Volunteer, Peace Corps staff response may include reassessing the Volunteer's worksite and housing arrangements and making any adjustments, as needed. In some cases, the nature of the incident may necessitate a site or housing transfer. Peace Corps staff will also assist Volunteers with preserving their rights to pursue legal sanctions against the perpetrators of the crime. It is very important that Volunteers report incidents as they occur, not only to protect their peer Volunteers, but also to preserve the future right to prosecute. Should Volunteers decide later in the process that they want to proceed with the prosecution of their assailant, this option may no longer exist if the evidence of the event has not been preserved at the time of the incident.

In March 2003, the Peace Corps created the Office of Safety and Security. Its mission is to "foster improved communication, coordination, oversight, and accountability of all Peace Corps' safety and security efforts."

The major responsibilities of the Volunteer Safety and Overseas Security Division are to coordinate the office's overseas operations and direct the Peace Corps' safety and security officers who are located in various regions around the world that have Peace Corps programs. The safety and security officers conduct security assessments; review safety trainings; train trainers and managers; train Volunteer safety wardens, local guards, and staff; develop security incident response procedures; and provide crisis management support.

If a trainee or Volunteer is the victim of a safety incident, Peace Corps staff is prepared to provide support. All Peace Corps posts have procedures in place to respond to incidents of crime committed against Volunteers. The first priority for all posts in the aftermath of an incident is to ensure that the Volunteer is safe and receiving medical treatment as needed. After assuring the safety of the Volunteer, Peace Corps staff members provide support by reassessing a Volunteer's worksite and housing arrangements and making any adjustments, as needed. In some cases, the nature of the incident may necessitate a project site or housing transfer. Peace Corps staff will also assist Volunteers with preserving their rights to pursue legal sanctions against the perpetrators of the crime. It is very important that Volunteers report incidents as they occur, not only to protect their peer Volunteers, but also to preserve the future right to prosecute.

Crime Data for the Dominican Republic

Crime data and statistics for the Dominican Republic, which is updated yearly, are available at the following link: http://www.peacecorps.gov/countrydata/dominicanrepublic

Please take the time to review this important information.

Few Peace Corps Volunteers are victims of serious crimes and crimes that do occur overseas are investigated and prosecuted by local authorities through the local courts system. If you are the victim of a crime, you will decide if you wish to pursue prosecution. If you decide to prosecute, Peace Corps will be there to assist you. One of our tasks is to ensure you are fully informed of your options and understand how the local legal process works. Peace Corps will help you ensure your rights are protected to the fullest extent possible under the laws of the country.

If you are the victim of a serious crime, you will learn how to get to a safe location as quickly as possible and contact your Peace Corps office. It's important that you notify Peace Corps as soon as you can so Peace Corps can provide you with the help you need.

Volunteer Safety Support in the Dominican Republic

Preparing for the Unexpected: Safety Training and Volunteer Support in the Dominican Republic
The Peace Corps' approach to safety is a five-pronged plan to help you stay safe during your two-year service and includes the following: Information sharing, Volunteer training, site selection criteria, a detailed emergency action plan, and protocols for reporting and responding to safety and security incidents. the Dominican Republic's in-country safety program is outlined below.

The Peace Corps/Dominican Republic office will keep Volunteers informed of any issues that may impact Volunteer safety through **information sharing**. Regular updates will be provided in Volunteer newsletters and in memorandums from the country director. In the event of a critical situation or emergency, Volunteers will be contacted through the emergency communication network.

Volunteer training will include sessions on specific safety and security issues in the Dominican Republic. This training will prepare you to adopt a culturally appropriate lifestyle and exercise judgment that promotes safety and reduces risk in your home, at work, and while traveling. Safety training is offered throughout service and is integrated into the language, cross-cultural, health, and other components of training.

Certain **site selection criteria** are used to determine safe housing for Volunteers before their arrival. The Peace Corps staff works closely with host communities and counterpart agencies to help prepare them for a Volunteer's arrival and to establish expectations of their respective roles in supporting the Volunteer. Each site is inspected before the Volunteer's arrival to ensure placement in appropriate, safe, and secure housing and work sites. Site selection is based in part on any relevant site history; access to medical, banking, postal, and other essential services; availability of communications, transportation, and markets; different housing options and living arrangements; and other Volunteer support needs.

You will also learn about Peace Corps/Dominican Republic's **detailed emergency action plan**, which is implemented in the event of civil or political unrest or a natural disaster. When you arrive at your site, you will complete and submit a site locator form with your address, contact information, and a map to your house. If there is a security threat, Volunteers in the Dominican Republic will gather at predetermined locations until the situation is resolved or the Peace Corps decides to evacuate.

Finally, in order for the Peace Corps to be fully responsive to the needs of Volunteers, it is imperative that Volunteers **immediately report** any security incident to the Peace Corps Safety and Security Coordinator. The Peace Corps has established protocols for addressing safety and security incidents in a timely and appropriate manner, and it collects and evaluates safety and security data to track trends and develop strategies to minimize risks to future Volunteers.

DIVERSITY AND CROSS-CULTURAL ISSUES

In fulfilling its mandate to share the face of America with host countries, the Peace Corps is making special efforts to assure that all of America's richness is reflected in the Volunteer corps. More Americans of color are serving in today's Peace Corps than at any time in recent history. Differences in race, ethnic background, age, religion, and sexual orientation are expected and welcomed among our Volunteers. Part of the Peace Corps' mission is to help dispel any notion that Americans are all of one origin or race and to establish that each of us is as thoroughly American as the other despite our many differences.

Our diversity helps us accomplish that goal. In other ways, however, it poses challenges. In the Dominican Republic, as in other Peace Corps host countries, Volunteers' behavior, lifestyle, background, and beliefs are judged in a cultural context very different from their own. Certain personal perspectives or characteristics commonly accepted in the United States may be quite uncommon, unacceptable, or even repressed in the Dominican Republic.

Outside of the Dominican Republic's capital, residents of rural communities have had relatively little direct exposure to other cultures, races, religions, and lifestyles. What people view as typical American behavior or norms may be a misconception, such as the belief that all Americans are rich and have blond hair and blue eyes. The people of the Dominican Republic are justly known for their generous hospitality to foreigners; however, members of the community in which you will live may display a range of reactions to cultural differences that you present.

To ease the transition and adapt to life in the Dominican Republic, you may need to make some temporary, yet fundamental compromises in how you present yourself as an American and as an individual. For example, female trainees and Volunteers may not be able to exercise the independence available to them in the United States; political discussions need to be handled with great care; and some of your personal beliefs may best remain undisclosed. You will need to develop techniques and personal strategies for coping with these and other limitations. The Peace Corps staff will lead diversity and sensitivity discussions during pre-service training and will be on call to provide support, but the challenge ultimately will be your own.

Overview of Diversity in the Dominican Republic

The Peace Corps staff in the Dominican Republic recognizes the adjustment issues that come with diversity and will endeavor to provide support and guidance. During pre-service training, several sessions will be held to discuss diversity and coping mechanisms. We look forward to having male and female Volunteers from a variety of races, ethnic groups, ages, religions, and sexual orientations, and hope that you will become part of a diverse group of Americans who take pride in supporting one another and demonstrating the richness of American culture.

What Might a Volunteer Face?

Possible Issues for Female Volunteers

Female Volunteers should know that Dominican society has elements of machismo. Men often hiss and make comments to women walking by, and women must learn to deal with this by completely ignoring men who behave in this way. Most female Volunteers never fully accept this sexual harassment, but they develop a tolerance within which they are able to function effectively. Dating for American women in the Dominican Republic is also a sensitive subject. The Dominican culture follows its own guidelines as it relates to male-female relationships; for example, female Volunteers who live alone should not invite males into their homes unless they have intentions of beginning a serious relationship with the man.

Volunteer Comments

"Being a woman in the Dominican Republic is sometimes frustrating. This is a patriarchal society that treats women much like America did pre-1960s. It helps that three Peace Corps women have successfully served before me in my community, and the elders recognize the contributions that we, as women, are making. It's also an inspiration to see the women of the community empowered by the women's leadership conference several Volunteers co-sponsored last year. Change here is slow, but I definitely see the society evolving. It's sometimes difficult to put my American attitude of gender equality aside, but I keep reminding myself that I am here to share their culture as much as I am here to share mine with them."

"My experience in the Dominican Republic has both tamed and fueled the feminist in me. I realized when I got to my site that I wasn't going to be productive by starting the 'foreigner's feminist movement' in the Dominican Republic. Since alcoholism among men here is high, women in the Dominican Republic seem to carry the larger burden, but you'll never hear them complaining. I like working at the grassroots level, sponsoring workshops for women in coordination with our Women in Development committee. We are working with the younger generation, raising young women's self-esteem and trying to change their perceptions of women's importance in the community."

"Not only am I a woman in the Dominican Republic, I am a young, single, childless, and extremely independent woman. These are traits rarely seen in Dominican women and often misunderstood by Dominican men. However, these traits also allow me to express my individualism and self-pride. Yes, I experience unwanted attention from men and, in extreme cases, a few annoying admirers. But these situations allow me to face sexism and disrespect head-on by educating the violators about why women should be looked upon as equals to their male counterparts. It also helps that I'm from America and I've faced similar challenges there. Therefore, being a feminist (but not to the extreme) in the D.R. attracts respect from both men and women. I also get the opportunity to educate and help young girls build confidence in themselves. I suggest that female Volunteers exude confidence and their ability to perform as integral parts of society. And if it gets too frustrating, you have a support team of over 60 American women (Peace Corps staff and fellow Volunteers) to tell you why you are strong and phenomenal!"

Possible Issues for Volunteers of Color
In rural sites and even in some cities, a Volunteer is usually the only foreign resident and receives extra attention, especially because of his or her racial or ethnic background. Volunteers in certain areas of the country are more prone to racial discrimination than others. African-American Volunteers in the northwest or near the Haitian border, for example, may be asked for their passports. Most Volunteers of color say that despite initial confusion regarding their nationality and discrimination, they are well-received in their communities.

African-American Volunteers may face some unique challenges. They are sometimes mistaken for Dominicans or Haitians. If seen as Dominican, this can lead to an expectation of Spanish fluency; if seen as Haitian, it can result in poor treatment by Dominicans. African-American Volunteers should be prepared to face mild cases of discrimination and racism. However, Volunteers should remain open-minded and calm. Many of these situations are due to lack of education and the history of the Dominican Republic. On the other hand, misidentification with black ethnic groups other than Haitians, such as members of the English-speaking Eastern Caribbean population, may lead to faster acceptance. Female African-American Volunteers should also be prepared to face issues concerning their hair. The straightness of a woman's hair is considered an important quality by many. Though natural hairstyles are accepted, they are not as highly looked upon as straight hair. Relaxers, usually manufactured locally, are available for Volunteers who wish to use them. U.S. brand name hair products may be available but they may be more expensive.

Hispanic-American Volunteers may be surprised to find that some Dominicans are unaware that not all Hispanic Americans are of Mexican origin. Because there is a small population of Dominicans of South Asian descent, some Asian-American Volunteers have been misidentified as Dominicans, especially in urban areas.

Volunteer Comments

"I am one of the African-American Volunteers in the Dominican Republic. There are stares and giggles, which is quite disconcerting. Many people believe you are from Africa. Most people have been very nice and have opened up their homes to me. Many people believe that there are no races of people other than Caucasians living in the United States. I really believe my presence is an educational experience for the community. I would do it again. People here are very hospitable; they want to meet and get to know you. There are no special products for hair and skin care for African Americans, so load up your bags or send packages through the mail. I am having a great time at my site. The community really wants to know what America is like."

Locally-produced hair and skin products are readily available in stores for Volunteers who wish to use them. U.S. brand names are available at high-end beauty salons or stores located in the two largest cities in the country (Santo Domingo and Santiago). They may be hard to find in communities where volunteers serve and much more expensive than local products."

"Pride, self-love, confidence ... Just some of the things that get me through a normal day in the Dominican Republic. Similar to every country in the world (including the United States), racism exists in the D.R., whether it's between the D.R.'s neighbors (Haitians), visitors (tourists of color), or themselves. I've made it a part of my mission as an African-American Volunteer to bring awareness to fellow Volunteers and the Dominican community, as well as to support other diverse Volunteers with their struggles against racism. I've begun to praise the color of skin, appreciate the history of my people, educate the Dominicans of my community, acknowledge the differences in society, and love myself even more. As Volunteers, we take on a task to shed all that is familiar and comfortable and experience what is different and disturbing. For me, some days are more challenging than others, but every day counts. So, every day I wake up thankful for the color of my skin, the texture of my hair, and my commitment to fighting the cause another day."

"Being a Mexican-American Volunteer in northern Dominican Republic has been a positive experience. People have been very welcoming and interested in my family's traditions. At first, they figured they knew everything about my heritage because most are quite familiar with the images of Mexico and Mexicans presented on the dubbed Mexican soaps that are all the rage here. Sometimes when I tell people I'm Mexican American, I get an excited reaction: 'Oh! Like Veronica Castro!' I brought postcards and pictures of Mexico, which have been a hit."

"I wouldn't say I have had problems as an Asian-American Volunteer. A few people are surprised when they discover I'm American and have said, for example, 'You don't look American.' For the most part, though, being Asian has been more of a positive than a negative. There are many places where I can go where I won't and don't stand out."

Possible Issues for Senior Volunteers

Approximately 5 percent of Volunteers in the Dominican Republic are seniors. The vast majority of other people in the Peace Corps community are in their 20s. Service in the Dominican Republic can present significant social and logistical issues for senior Volunteers. Dealing with family emergencies, maintaining lifelong friendships, and arranging Power of Attorney for financial matters may be more problematic for older Volunteers than younger ones. Still, older Volunteers find Dominicans, the Peace Corps staff, and fellow Volunteers to be very welcoming.

Volunteer Comments

"I love it! In fact, when I went home for a vacation, I was suddenly confronted with age discrimination. Here in the Dominican Republic, I was constantly treated with respect. I was never hassled by men on the streets, almost always given a seat on the bus, and given an inordinate amount of respect by younger people. The Volunteers were great, and although I am over 60, one of my best friends is 22. Oh, and my health has never been better. Walking everywhere brought my cholesterol levels down to below average, my body is almost in shape (I lost about 40 pounds), and I feel 20 years younger than I did before I joined the Peace Corps."

"I have not experienced negative issues at my site from either Volunteers or work associates. I feel I have been accepted on all levels and included in local and Volunteer activities and socializing. Training was a little uncomfortable. I felt generational differences at the time, but it may have been largely the tension of attending concentrated training in a sizable group such as ours. Personal support from the Volunteers at my site is always available and very warmly and sincerely offered."

Possible Issues for Gay, Lesbian, or Bisexual Volunteers

Homosexual or bisexual Volunteers are not able to express their sexual orientation as openly as they may have in the United States because of cultural differences and machismo in the Dominican Republic. Because of prejudice against homosexuals in Dominican society, it is wise to know your community and co-workers well before disclosing your sexual orientation.

While there are certainly homosexuals in the Dominican Republic, they do not have the level of acceptance found in much of the United States. Although some Dominicans consider homosexuality immoral, their view of homosexuality among foreigners may be quite different from their view of homosexuality among nationals. Styles of hair and clothes and earrings on men may be considered inappropriate by Dominicans.

Most Dominican homosexuals probably have migrated to larger cities, but many Peace Corps Volunteers are posted in small communities. Relationships with homosexual or bisexual host country nationals can happen, but as with other cross-cultural relationships, they may not be easy.

Volunteer Comments

"Know that you may face additional challenges as a gay, lesbian, or bisexual Volunteer. But we have to remember that making sacrifices is part of being a Peace Corps Volunteer. I can say that having to 'go back into the closet' in my community has been one of the biggest challenges of my service thus far. The best advice I can give to gay Volunteers coming to the Dominican Republic is to find support within the Peace Corps/Dominican Republic community right away. I've found that most of the administrative, training, and health staff, as well as other Volunteers, have been very supportive. Remember that you don't have to completely hide your identity, but it's going to take some time and may be challenging to find healthy and socially acceptable ways to express it. Be patient with yourself and Dominican culture."

"Living a white lie is, unfortunately, a part of everyday life. In the beginning, this idea of not completely sharing my life with host country nationals appeared to be something I could tolerate. However, as time passed I started to build close friendships and would like to share my life with people on a more personal level. To avoid rejection and social problems in my town, I have chosen to keep my lifestyle to myself. For such reasons and to put a stop to the constant questions about my love life (everyone wants to know why someone in his mid-20s has not married yet), saying that a close Volunteer friend of mine is really my girlfriend put a stop to the uncomfortable questions."

"There is a small gay community in the capital. Their lifestyle is very secretive and they keep to themselves. I've decided to not associate with these people to avoid raising suspicion. Everyone seems to know one another, and gossip travels quickly."

Possible Religious Issues for Volunteers

Volunteers are frequently asked about their religious affiliation and may be invited to attend a community church. Volunteers not in the practice of attending church may be challenged to explain their reluctance, but it is possible to politely decline if the church or religion is not one of your choice. Most Volunteers find effective ways to cope with this and feel quite at home in the Dominican Republic.

Volunteer Comment

"I've never really been too religious in my life, and certainly never tried to persuade someone to be a certain way. So it was a little strange for me when I arrived at my site and had many of my neighbors asking what religion I was, whether I went to church on Sundays, and how well I knew the Bible. My first few weeks, I didn't attend church on Sundays—unlike just about everyone in town—and felt like a pariah. The services would last for hours. Well, I developed a strategy of going for about the first hour or so, showing my face, and then splitting. Even though I felt a little odd doing this, I found that my community opened up more to me and to the projects I had developed. I wouldn't recommend what I did to everyone, but my compromise seemed to help me."

Possible Issues for Volunteers With Disabilities

As a disabled Volunteer in the Dominican Republic, you may find that you face a special set of challenges. In the Dominican Republic, as in other parts of the world, some people may hold prejudicial attitudes about individuals with disabilities and may discriminate against them. What is more, there is very little of the infrastructure to accommodate individuals with disabilities that has been developed in the United States.

However, as part of the medical clearance process, the Peace Corps Office of Medical Services determined that you were physically and emotionally capable, with or without reasonable accommodations, to perform a full tour of Volunteer service in the Dominican Republic without unreasonable risk of harm to yourself or interruption of your service. The Peace Corps/Dominican Republic staff will work with disabled Volunteers to make reasonable accommodations in training, housing, job sites, or other areas to enable them to serve safely and effectively.

Possible Issues for Married Volunteers

Being a married couple in the Peace Corps has its advantages and its challenges. It helps to have someone by your side to share your experience with, but there are also cultural expectations that can cause stress in a marriage. It is important to remember that you are in a foreign country with new rules and you need to be open-minded about cultural differences. A couple may have to take on some new roles.

A married man may be encouraged by Dominicans to be the more dominant member in the relationship, be encouraged to make decisions independently of his spouse, or be ridiculed when he performs domestic tasks. A married woman may find herself in a less independent role than she is accustomed to or may be expected to perform "traditional" domestic chores such as cooking or cleaning. She may also experience a more limited social life in the community than single Volunteers (since it may be assumed that she will be busy taking care of her husband). Competition may become a difficulty, especially if one spouse learns faster than the other (e.g., language skills, job skills). There also may be differences in job satisfaction and/or different needs between spouses. Younger Volunteers may look to couples for advice and support. Married couples also are likely to be treated with more respect because the community sees marriage as a responsibility. They may be asked when they are going to have children.

FREQUENTLY ASKED QUESTIONS

How much luggage am I allowed to bring to The Dominican Republic?

Most airlines have baggage size and weight limits and assess charges for transport of baggage that exceeds those limits. The Peace Corps has its own size and weight limits and will not pay the cost of transport for baggage that exceeds these limits. The Peace Corps' allowance is two checked pieces of luggage with combined dimensions of both pieces not to exceed 107 inches (length + width + height) and a carry-on bag with dimensions of no more than 45 inches. Checked baggage should not exceed 80 pounds total with a maximum weight of 50 pounds for any one bag.

Peace Corps Volunteers are not allowed to take pets, weapons, explosives, radio transmitters (shortwave radios are permitted), automobiles, or motorcycles to their overseas assignments. Do not pack flammable materials or liquids such as lighter fluid, cleaning solvents, hair spray, or aerosol containers. This is an important safety precaution.

What is the electric current in The Dominican Republic?

It is 110 volts, 60 cycles (similar to that in the United States). Many Volunteers do not have electricity in their houses or have it for only a few hours a day.

How much money should I bring?

Volunteers are expected to live at the same level as the people in their community. You will be given a settling-in allowance and a monthly living allowance, which should cover your expenses. Volunteers often wish to bring additional money for vacation travel to other countries. Credit cards and traveler's checks are preferable to cash. If you choose to bring extra money, bring the amount that will suit your own travel plans and needs.

When can I take vacation and have people visit me?

Each Volunteer accrues two vacation days per month of service (excluding training). Leave may not be taken during training, the first three months of service, or the last three months of service, except in conjunction with an authorized emergency leave. Family and friends are welcome to visit you after pre-service training and the first three months of service as long as their stay does not interfere with your work. Extended stays at your site are not encouraged and may require permission from your country director. The Peace Corps is not able to provide your visitors with visa, medical, or travel assistance.

Will my belongings be covered by insurance?

The Peace Corps does not provide insurance coverage for personal effects; Volunteers are ultimately responsible for the safekeeping of their personal belongings. However, you can purchase personal property insurance before you leave. If you wish, you may contact your own insurance company; additionally, insurance application forms will be provided, and we encourage you to consider them carefully. Volunteers should not ship or take valuable items overseas. Jewelry, watches, radios, cameras, and expensive appliances are subject to loss, theft, and breakage, and in many places, satisfactory maintenance and repair services are not available.

Do I need an international driver's license?

Volunteers in the Dominican Republic do not need an international driver's license because they are prohibited from operating privately owned motorized vehicles. Most urban travel is by bus or taxi. Rural travel ranges from buses and minibuses to trucks, bicycles, and lots of walking. On very rare occasions, a Volunteer may be asked to drive a sponsor's vehicle, but this can occur only with prior written permission from the country director. Should this occur, the Volunteer may obtain a local driver's license. A U.S. driver's license will facilitate the process, so bring it with you just in case.

What should I bring as gifts for Dominican Republic friends and my host family?

This is not a requirement. A token of friendship is sufficient. Some gift suggestions include knickknacks for the house; pictures, books, or calendars of American scenes; souvenirs from your area; hard candies that will not melt or spoil; or photos to give away.

Where will my site assignment be when I finish training and how isolated will I be?

Peace Corps trainees are not assigned to individual sites until after they have completed pre-service training. This gives Peace Corps staff the opportunity to assess each trainee's technical and language skills prior to assigning sites, in addition to finalizing site selections with their ministry counterparts. If feasible, you may have the opportunity to provide input on your site preferences, including geographical location, distance from other Volunteers, and living conditions. However, keep in mind that many factors influence the site selection process and that the Peace Corps cannot guarantee placement where you would ideally like to be. Most Volunteers live in small towns or in rural villages and are usually within one hour from another Volunteer. Some sites require a 10- to 12-hour drive from the capital. There is at least one Volunteer based in each of the regional capitals and about five to eight Volunteers in the capital city.

How can my family contact me in an emergency?

The Peace Corps' Office of Special Services provides assistance in handling emergencies affecting trainees and Volunteers or their families. Before leaving the United States, instruct your family to notify the Office of Special Services immediately if an emergency arises, such as a serious illness or death of a family member. During normal business hours, the number for the Office of Special Services is 800.424.8580; select option 2, then extension 1470. After normal business hours and on weekends and holidays, the Special Services duty officer can be reached at the above number. For non-emergency questions, your family can get information from your country desk staff at the Peace Corps by calling 800.424.8580.

Can I call home from the Dominican Republic?

Yes, you can call the United States easily from the Dominican Republic. Many businesses sell calling cards that work with any phone.

Should I bring a cellular phone with me?

You do not need to bring a cellular telephone with you; Peace Corps/Dominican Republic issues a cellphone to each Volunteer to ensure efficient communication with staff. Your phone can also be used to call internationally or locally by using a calling card; however, not all areas of the country currently have cellphone service

Will there be email and Internet access?

Many communities have computer centers or Internet cafes that provide email and Internet access, and the resource center at the Peace Corps/Dominican Republic office has computers for Volunteer use. It is a good idea to set up a Hotmail or Yahoo! account before you leave the United States so you have an email address family and friends can use to contact you in the Dominican Republic.

WELCOME LETTERS FROM DOMINICAN REPUBLIC VOLUNTEERS

WELCOME LETTERS FROM DOMINICAN REPUBLIC VOLUNTEERS

Bienvenidos a la República Dominicana!. You are moments away from embarking on a once-in-a-lifetime experience. I am a healthy families Volunteer in a campo outside of Santiago. As a part of my project, I work with youth promoting HIV/AIDS awareness and prevention. I also work with women to promote nutrition and reproductive health. Additional projects include a gravity-powered aqueduct, a birth certificate declaration campaign, and summer camps. Aside from my title as Volunteer/*profesora*, my community regards me as a daughter, sister, aunt, niece, godmother, neighbor, and friend, among other titles. The best thing that happened to me (which I hope you also experience) was the embracing of the culture and the people who occupy this island. Only then will you truly attain all that your time here has to offer.

The next two years (*por lo menos*) of your life will be filled with emotional highs and lows, hopefully more of the former than the latter. The best advice I can give you is to take experiences and people as they come. It is very easy to compare and contrast your life in the Dominican Republic with that of your life in the United States ... DON'T DO IT! You are not in the States and what works here may not work there and vice versa. *Cojéelo Suave*, or take it easy and keep an open mind, you'll be amazed with what you learn and who you meet. Throw caution, although NOT ALL, to the wind and try new things in the name of "cultural immersion." You'll find that you like most things and can excuse yourself, in the future, from those you don't with the excuse that you have already tried it, and nine times out of 10 you will have a great story to tell friends and family back home.

Cuídese y que disfrute todo (Take care and enjoy everything)

—Marita Lamb

I found the transition from self-employment and teaching in the United States to be quite smooth. I divested myself of most of my material possessions and financial obligations (my home, vehicles, debts) and followed the urge to gain a new and different experience. I do not regret my decision at all. It has been good for me emotionally, intellectually, and physically. I do not feel that I have severed relationships at home, either. In part, I am pursuing Peace Corps as a new beginning, a sort of professional development activity focused upon my desire to become proficient in Spanish. I believe that my experience here will make me more marketable should I decide to apply for public school teaching positions or social service work when I return home.

I have been welcomed as a peer by my group, most of whom are in their 20s, and I enjoy their company immensely. To look out from this 58-year-old frame and to be surrounded by exuberant and intelligent young people makes me feel younger than my years. I have tried not to play the part of the old know-it-all, following the lead of the young people most of the time. As a result, they include me in their activities and share their thoughts and concerns with me. Sometimes, believe it or not, they even solicit my opinion or advice. This is my second tour in the Peace Corps and I know that I am establishing lifelong friendships just as I did 35 years ago in Afghanistan. I can't wait for OUR reunions.

The transition to Dominican culture is not without a bump in the road now and then. Caribbean Spanish can be puzzling. This is a bustling and often noisy society and newcomers discover differences between the American and the Dominican work ethics. However, becoming accustomed to these things is a part of the learning experience. There are many wonderful Dominicans who sincerely want to help and befriend Americans and to learn from us. They are also capable of teaching us more than a little about life, family, and friendship.

—Ed Crawford

Saludos!

You probably joined the Peace Corps because you want to help change the world. Ironically, you are about to embark on an adventure that will change you forever. You have the opportunity to make an immeasurable impact on the lives of the community members where you will live and work. They will remember you and how you helped them for years to come. However, also be prepared to receive as much as you give. People will be unbelievably generous with the little that they have. Your experiences will shape you in ways that you never expected. Never again will you take for granted dependable electricity, mail delivery, or educational opportunities. It may even surprise you that after awhile, you are content without many things you considered "necessities." You will begin to understand the Peace Corps Slogan "The toughest job you'll ever love."

—Erica Giljohann

¡*Bienvenidas y bienvenidos*! Congratulations. You're in and you're headed to the Dominican Republic. This is a fantastic place to live and work. Surely you can inspire some healthy envy among your friends by telling them that you're off to live in the Dominican Republic for two years. Perhaps you can convince them to come and visit, to take the edge off their envy.

I know I had no idea what to expect, essentially, before I began life in Peace Corps over a year ago. I had profound doubts about joining the Peace Corps. You may also. But before you start your two years of service, you will spend three intense months with a group of extraordinary people learning Dominican Spanish (what's a *kakata*?), Dominican history, and technical skills to serve you in your work. You'll have a group of close friends to help you negotiate the cultural minefield or to laugh with you at your absurd mistakes (or better, their absurd mistakes).

Then, suddenly, your three months of training are up and they send you to your community. You're on your own. And if there is just one piece of advice I have, it is this: Life as a Volunteer is what you make of it. You are often hours and hours from your supervisors. Many people in your community have a vague idea of just who you are and what you are capable of. Stick to what you're good at and what you really like doing. You can find ways to meet project goals in innovative ways, without following a "template" for what a Volunteer is supposed to do. Not a single project is exactly like another one, they are all unique.

What can I tell you about my experience now? I am a basic and special education Volunteer in the central Cibao valley. I split my time between helping the elementary school develop effective literacy programs and helping the community establish a new school for kids with special needs. I aim to connect the community to existing resources. Specific technical skills are less valuable than persistence, thinking creatively, and trying to apply what works well in other places. The less I do and the more folks in town do, the better, from my perspective.

In my downtime, I do my best to improve my bachata and merengue dancing. I must report, shamefully, that I just don't have the ingrained rhythm that Dominicans do. When I need to retreat from life as a town spectacle, I dig around in my backyard, among the coconut, grapefruit, mandarins, noni, guava, marañon, and crabapples (all in a fairly small yard). And, of course, there's always a gorgeous white sandy Caribbean beach less than an hour down the road to keep my friends back home jealous.

—Neal Riemer

Felicidades! You don't know it yet, but you're about to embark on one of the most exciting, crazy, backward adventures of your life. One that will open your eyes, change your perspective, and make you question everything you ever thought to be true. The thrill of entering into a new country and a new culture and the challenge of speaking a new language make the dull moments seem exciting and the exciting moments, well you can only imagine!

I'm a youth families and community development Volunteer. I have been living in a rural village in southwest Dominican Republic for about 1 1/2 years now. I've worked on projects ranging from building a youth center, to teaching sex education, to helping citizens attain birth certificates, to doing reforestation projects. That's what's so great about the Peace Corps. It's a flexible job that lets you step outside of the box. You can design your projects to meet your community's needs while stimulating your own interests.

Some weeks seem like a steep uphill climb with no end in sight. The road is often long and bumpy with few straightaways and less road signs marking the way. But not knowing what's around the corner makes it exciting and challenging and makes each success that much sweeter.

I've learned how to carry water on my head, play dominos by candlelight, cook exotic dishes (rice and beans ... what's more exotic than that?), drink cafecito like a pro, and dance Bachata until dawn. You can't learn that in the States. And there is no emotional high greater than knowing you've improved someone's life, and where better to do it then the beautiful Caribbean island of the Dominican Republic? *Bienvenidos*!

—Jennifer Bires

PACKING LIST

This list has been compiled by Volunteers serving in The Dominican Republic and is based on their experience. Use it as an informal guide in making your own list, bearing in mind that each experience is individual. There is no perfect list! You obviously cannot bring everything on the list, so consider those items that make the most sense to you personally and professionally. You can always have things sent to you later. As you decide what to bring, keep in mind that you have an 80-pound weight limit on baggage. And remember, you can get almost everything you need in the Dominican Republic.

Clothing

During training, Peace Corps events, and some of your work activities, you should wear "business casual" clothing. In the context of Peace Corps/Dominican Republic, this would include, but is not limited to: nice jeans (no tears), khakis, business slacks, knee-length skirts/dresses for women, button-up shirts, polo shirts, shirts/blouses that cover the top of the shoulder for women, and nice sandals or close-toed shoes. We suggest you pack:

- One or two business casual outfits. If you are a community economic development or education Volunteer, consider bringing three or four outfits, but remember you can always buy clothes in the DR; 1 dressy outfit for swearing-in ceremony
- Three to five pairs of jeans/casual pants (or capris for women) for everyday work
- One or two pair of shorts for jogging/sports (not too short)
- At least five T-shirts/everyday shirts
- Two-week supply of underwear(cotton is highly recommended)
- Appropriate mix of work and dress socks (one-week supply)
- One to three swimsuits
- Two sweatshirts
- Rain jacket and/or umbrella
- Hat (baseball hats are popular in the DR)
- One or two belts
- Several small yet sturdy locks that you can put on your suitcases/bags/backpacks (Given the openness of the homes, PC/DR asks you to keep valuables locked inside a bag at all times)

Men: One or two ties (for special occasions like swearing-in ceremony), two to four pair of shorts

Women: Two to four pairs of shorts (it is recommended that women are conservative with the shorts they wear while in site; consider bermuda shorts or those just above the knee and please note shorts are not acceptable during PC training events or while in the PC office), two to four casual dresses and/or skirts

Shoes

- One pair sturdy of walking/hiking shoes (Vibrams are recommended, but these could be sneakers)
- One pair athletic shoes
- At least one pair of sandals such as chacos/tevas/rainbows
- One pair dress shoes or one to three pairs of nice sandals (without heels) for women

Personal Hygiene and Toiletry Items

You can buy almost anything that is available in the United States in the Dominican Republic. However, if you have any favorite brands of toiletries or cosmetics, you may want to bring a supply, as most imported items are considerably more expensive here than in the United States.

- Start-up supply of shampoo, deodorant, etc.
- One bath towel and one "quick dry" towel
- Women: several months supply of tampons (two Diva Cups are recommended because tampons are expensive and only sold in pharmacies)
- Contact lens solution (Peace Corps recommends that you use regular glasses, however, in the event that you do decide to use contacts, the solution is very expensive in the DR)

Kitchen
You can easily buy most kitchen supplies (e.g., dishes, pots, glasses, and utensils) locally. There are a few items you might consider bringing:

- An assortment of Ziploc bags
- One or two Tupperware containers
- Sturdy can opener
- Favorite spice(some are available here but expensive)
- Peeler
- Set of measuring cups/spoons

Electronics & Entertainment
Please keep in mind that many Dominicans in the areas where you will be living do not have and cannot afford expensive electronics like iPods and computers. If you are considering bringing items on this list, you should purchase personal articles insurance as these high-priced electronics may be at risk of theft and/or loss. A good battery source is also recommended since most towns, including the neighborhoods of Santo Domingo, experience frequent and prolonged power outages.

- iPod/other music player (iTouches, and iPhones when put in airplane mode, can pick up wireless Internet at no charge. This can be very useful for Skype and they are more portable than a computer)
- Portable speakers with batteries
- Digital camera

- Rechargeable batteries and charger
- USB flash drive (external hard drives are highly recommended because many Volunteers use them for work purposes and to download movies and TV shows)
- A laptop computer with wireless access is HIGHLY recommended. Many Volunteers list this as the most useful thing they brought; netbooks or smaller laptops are also highly recommended
- Surge protector for electrical appliances

Miscellaneous

- One to two good quality water bottles (such as Nalgene)
- Sturdy backpack or bag for three- or four-day trips
- Back pack or day pack
- Money belt (Peace Corps will provide you with one, but if you have a preference on style/shape, bring your own)
- Queen-sized cotton sheets with pillowcases (it may be better to have these shipped after you know what mattress you will have for the next two years)
- Travel alarm clock
- Multiple-utility pocketknife (such as a Leatherman)
- Light, stuffable sleeping bag (this will be helpful for the times when you have to bring your own sheets to training events or if you live in a colder area you can unzip it and use it as a blanket)
- Yoga mat (if you practice yoga)
- Head lamps are highly recommended, especially if LED
- Sewing kit
- Start-up supply of stationary and pens
- Small/interesting games

Things Not To Bring

- English-Spanish Dictionary
- 501 Spanish Verbs book
- 101 Most Useful Spanish Words
- Too many books (while English books are hard to find in-country, the Peace Corps office has a LARGE variety of books that have been left by Volunteers over the years). The Peace Corps resource library is also quite extensive so we only recommended bringing resource manuals you find necessary to your work while in country
- Sunscreen and bug spray (these will be supplied by the medical once you have arrived)
- Too many clothes (remember, you will be changing host families three times during your first three months and much of what you have can probably be easily purchased here or shipped from home)
- High heel shoes

PRE-DEPARTURE CHECKLIST

The following list consists of suggestions for you to consider as you prepare to live outside the United States for two years. Not all items will be relevant to everyone, and the list does not include everything you should make arrangements for.

Family

- Notify family that they can call the Peace Corps' Office of Special Services at any time if there is a critical illness or death of a family member (24-hour telephone number: 800.424.8580, extension 1470).

- Give the Peace Corps' *On the Home Front* handbook to family and friends.

Passport/Travel

- Forward to the Peace Corps travel office all paperwork for the Peace Corps passport and visas.

- Verify that your luggage meets the size and weight limits for international travel.

- Obtain a personal passport if you plan to travel after your service ends. (Your Peace Corps passport will expire three months after you finish your service, so if you plan to travel longer, you will need a regular passport.)

Medical/Health

- Complete any needed dental and medical work.

- If you wear glasses, bring two pairs.

- Arrange to bring a three-month supply of all medications (including birth control pills) you are currently taking.

Insurance

- Make arrangements to maintain life insurance coverage.

- Arrange to maintain supplemental health coverage while you are away. (Even though the Peace Corps is responsible for your health care during Peace Corps service overseas, it is advisable for people who have pre-existing conditions to arrange for the continuation of their supplemental health coverage. If there is a lapse in coverage, it is often difficult and expensive to be reinstated.)

- Arrange to continue Medicare coverage if applicable.

Personal Papers

- Bring a copy of your certificate of marriage or divorce.

Voting
- Register to vote in the state of your home of record. (Many state universities consider voting and payment of state taxes as evidence of residence in that state.)

- Obtain a voter registration card and take it with you overseas.

- Arrange to have an absentee ballot forwarded to you overseas.

Personal Effects
- Purchase personal property insurance to extend from the time you leave your home for service overseas until the time you complete your service and return to the United States.

Financial Management
- Keep a bank account in your name in the U.S.

- Obtain student loan deferment forms from the lender or loan service.

- Execute a Power of Attorney for the management of your property and business.

- Arrange for deductions from your readjustment allowance to pay alimony, child support, and other debts through the Office of Volunteer Financial Operations at 800.424.8580, extension 1770.

- Place all important papers—mortgages, deeds, stocks, and bonds—in a safe deposit box or with an attorney or other caretaker.

CONTACTING PEACE CORPS HEADQUARTERS

This list of numbers will help connect you with the appropriate office at Peace Corps headquarters to answer various questions. You can use the toll-free number and extension or dial directly using the local numbers provided. Be sure to leave the toll-free number and extensions with your family so they can contact you in the event of an emergency.

Peace Corps Headquarters Toll-free Number: 800.424.8580, Press 2, Press 1, then Ext. # (see below)

Peace Corps' Mailing Address: Peace Corps
Paul D. Coverdell Peace Corps Headquarters
1111 20th Street, NW
Washington, DC 20526

For Questions About:	Staff:	Toll-Free Ext:	Direct/Local Number:
Responding to an Invitation:			
	Office of Placement	x1840	202.692.1840
Country Information	Jennifer Mayo	x2509	202.692.2509
	Desk Officer / jmayo@peacecorps.gov		
Plane Tickets, Passports, Visas, or other travel matters:			
	SATO Travel	x1170	202.692.1170
Legal Clearance	Office of Placement	x1840	202.692.1840
Medical Clearance and Forms Processing (includes dental):			
	Screening Nurse	x1500	202.692.1500
Medical Reimbursements (handled by a subcontractor)			800.818.8772
Loan Deferments, Taxes, Financial Operations		x1770	202.692.1770
Readjustment Allowance Withdrawals, Power of Attorney, Staging (Pre-Departure Orientation), and Reporting Instructions:			
	Office of Staging	x1865	202.692.1865

Note: You will receive comprehensive information concerning hotel and flight arrangements three to five weeks prior to departure. This information is not available sooner.

Family Emergencies (to get information to a Volunteer overseas) *24 hours:*

| | Office of SpecialServices | x1470 | 202.692.1470 |